Best Lunchbox Recipes
FOR KIDS

Healthy, Happy, and Delicious: Lunchbox Recipes for Growing Kids

Copyright-All Rights Reserved

This book has copyright protection.You can use the book for personal purpose.You should not see,use,alter,distribute,quote,take excerpts or paraphrase in part or whole the material contained in this book without obtaining the permission of the author first.

Introduction

Welcome to "Best Lunchbox Recipes for Kids" - a culinary journey that transforms the everyday task of packing lunch into a delightful and nutritious adventure! As parents, caregivers, and champions of our children's health and happiness, we know that providing well-balanced, appealing, and wholesome meals is not only a daily challenge but also a heartfelt expression of love.

In this cookbook, we've gathered an array of creative, kid-approved lunchbox recipes that strike the perfect balance between taste, nutrition, and convenience. These recipes are designed to satisfy the pickiest of eaters while ensuring they get the essential nutrients they need to thrive. From colorful salads and savory wraps to scrumptious muffins and fun finger foods, our goal is to make lunchtime a joyful experience for both you and your little ones.

We understand that the lunchbox plays a vital role in a child's daily routine. It's not just a meal; it's a source of nourishment, a conversation starter, and a way to show you care. It's the place where children discover new flavors, textures, and culinary traditions. It's where they make friends and create fond memories around shared meals.

In "Best Lunchbox Recipes for Kids," you'll find recipes that are:

Nutrient-Rich: We believe that good food is the foundation of a healthy, happy childhood. Our recipes incorporate a variety of fresh ingredients to provide essential vitamins, minerals, and energy.

Kid-Friendly: We understand that kids can be a tough crowd when it comes to food. That's why we've crafted recipes that appeal to their taste buds, featuring familiar favorites and exciting new twists.

Easy to Prepare: We know that busy mornings are the norm, so our recipes are designed to be practical and time-efficient. Many can be made in advance or assembled quickly.

Creative and Fun: Food should be an adventure! We've included recipes that encourage creativity and exploration in the kitchen, helping your child develop a love for good food.

Customizable: We recognize that every child is unique, with their own tastes and dietary needs. Our recipes often come with variations and substitutions, allowing you to tailor them to your child's preferences.

So, whether you're a seasoned chef or just starting your culinary journey, "Best Lunchbox Recipes for Kids" is here to inspire you and simplify your daily lunchbox routine. Join us in the kitchen as we embark on a flavorful exploration of dishes that will not only nourish your child's body but also their spirit. Together, let's make lunchtime a delightful and memorable experience for your family.

Happy cooking and happy lunchboxing!

Lunchbox pasta salad

Ingredients:

For the Salad:
2 cups cooked pasta (such as rotini or penne), cooled
1 cup cherry tomatoes, halved
1/2 cup cucumber, diced
1/4 cup red onion, finely chopped
1/4 cup bell peppers (any color), diced
1/4 cup black olives, sliced
1/4 cup feta cheese, crumbled
2 tablespoons fresh basil leaves, chopped

For the Dressing:

3 tablespoons olive oil
2 tablespoons balsamic vinegar
1 teaspoon Dijon mustard
1 teaspoon honey
Salt and pepper to taste

Instructions:

Prepare the Dressing:
In a small bowl, whisk together the olive oil, balsamic vinegar, Dijon mustard, honey, salt, and pepper. Set aside.
In a large mixing bowl, combine the cooked pasta, cherry tomatoes, cucumber, red onion, bell peppers, black olives, and feta cheese.
Drizzle the dressing over the salad ingredients. Gently toss to coat everything evenly with the dressing.
Cover the bowl with plastic wrap or a lid and refrigerate the pasta salad for at least 30 minutes. This allows the flavors to meld and the pasta to absorb the dressing.
Before serving, sprinkle the chopped fresh basil leaves over the pasta salad. Give it a final toss to distribute the basil. Taste and adjust seasoning if needed.
Portion the pasta salad into lunch containers or bento boxes. Make sure to pack a fork or a small utensil for easy eating.
Whether at school, work, or on a picnic, your lunchbox pasta salad is ready to be enjoyed. The flavors will have melded beautifully, making every bite a burst of freshness and deliciousness.
This Lunchbox Pasta Salad recipe is a versatile option that combines the convenience of a packed lunch with the satisfaction of a wholesome, flavorful meal. It's a great way to bring a taste of summer to your lunch hour, all neatly packed and ready to enjoy!

Super-salad wraps

Ingredients:

For the Wraps:
4 whole wheat or spinach tortilla wraps
1 cup cooked quinoa, cooled
1 cup cooked and shredded chicken (or chickpeas for a vegetarian option)
1 cup mixed greens (spinach, kale, arugula)
1/2 cup cherry tomatoes, halved
1/4 cup red onion, thinly sliced
1/4 cup shredded carrots
1/4 cup cucumber, julienned
1/4 cup feta cheese, crumbled
2 tablespoons sunflower seeds or chopped nuts (optional)
Fresh herbs (such as parsley or cilantro), chopped

For the Dressing:

3 tablespoons olive oil
2 tablespoons lemon juice
1 teaspoon Dijon mustard
1 clove garlic, minced
Salt and pepper to taste

Instructions:

Prepare the Dressing:
In a small bowl, whisk together the olive oil, lemon juice, Dijon mustard, minced garlic, salt, and pepper. Set aside.
Lay out the tortilla wraps on a clean surface. Divide the cooked quinoa, shredded chicken (or chickpeas), mixed greens, cherry tomatoes, red onion, shredded carrots, cucumber, feta cheese, and sunflower seeds (if using) among the wraps.
Drizzle a generous spoonful of the prepared dressing over the ingredients on each wrap.
Carefully fold the sides of the tortilla wraps inwards, then roll them up tightly from the bottom, enclosing the filling.
Secure and Pack:
If needed, secure the wraps with a toothpick or wrap them in parchment paper to prevent them from unwrapping. Place the wraps in your lunchbox or bento box.
Garnish and Enjoy:
Before sealing the lunchbox, sprinkle chopped fresh herbs over the wraps for an extra burst of flavor. Seal the lunchbox and store it in the refrigerator until it's time to enjoy.
When it's time for lunch, unwrap your super-salad wraps and relish the mix of textures and flavors in each bite. These wraps are not only delicious but also a powerhouse of nutrients to keep you energized throughout the day.

Crunchy chopped salad

Ingredients:

For the Salad:
2 cups mixed greens (lettuce, spinach, or your choice)
1/2 cup cherry tomatoes, halved
1/4 cup cucumber, diced
1/4 cup bell peppers (any color), diced
1/4 cup carrots, shredded
1/4 cup cheddar cheese, cubed
1/4 cup cooked and diced chicken (optional for added protein)
1/4 cup croutons or whole-grain crackers, crushed

For the Creamy Ranch Dressing:

2 tablespoons plain Greek yogurt
1 tablespoon mayonnaise
1 teaspoon apple cider vinegar (or lemon juice)
1/2 teaspoon dried dill
1/4 teaspoon garlic powder

Instructions:

Prepare the Dressing:
In a small bowl, whisk together the Greek yogurt, mayonnaise, apple cider vinegar, dried dill, garlic powder, salt, and pepper until well combined. Taste and adjust seasoning as needed. Set aside.
In a larger container or lunchbox-friendly container, layer the mixed greens, cherry tomatoes, cucumber, bell peppers, shredded carrots, cheddar cheese, and diced chicken (if using).
Just before eating, sprinkle the crushed croutons or whole-grain crackers over the salad to add a satisfying crunch.
You can either pack the dressing in a separate small container or drizzle it over the salad just before eating - whichever is more convenient.
Seal the container and keep the salad cool in the refrigerator until lunchtime.

Lunchtime Enjoyment:
When it's time for lunch, drizzle the creamy ranch dressing over the crunchy chopped salad and toss to coat. Every bite will be a delightful combination of flavors and textures that your kids will love.
This Crunchy Chopped Salad is a lunchbox winner, filled with fresh and colorful ingredients that offer a delightful mix of flavors. The creamy ranch dressing adds a tangy kick, while the croutons or crackers provide that satisfying crunch. It's a wholesome and tasty option that your kids will look forward to devouring!

Easy egg muffins

Ingredients:

6 large eggs
1/4 cup milk
1/2 cup diced vegetables (bell peppers, spinach, tomatoes, etc.)
1/4 cup shredded cheddar cheese
Salt and pepper to taste
Cooking spray or muffin liners

Instructions:

Preheat the Oven:
Preheat your oven to 350°F (175°C). Lightly grease a muffin tin with cooking spray or line with muffin liners.
Prepare the Egg Mixture:
In a mixing bowl, whisk together the eggs and milk until well combined. Season with a pinch of salt and pepper.
Add Vegetables and Cheese:
Divide the diced vegetables and shredded cheddar cheese evenly among the muffin cups.
Pour Egg Mixture:
Pour the egg and milk mixture into each muffin cup, filling them about 2/3 full.
Bake the Egg Muffins:
Place the muffin tin in the preheated oven and bake for 15-20 minutes, or until the egg muffins are set and the tops are slightly golden.
Cool and Pack:
Once done, remove the egg muffins from the oven and let them cool in the muffin tin for a few minutes. Transfer the muffins to a wire rack to cool completely before packing them in the lunchbox.
Lunchbox Ready:
Pack the cooled egg muffins in the lunchbox along with any desired sides, such as whole-grain bread, fruit, or yogurt.
These easy egg muffins are versatile and delicious, providing a protein-packed option that's perfect for a kids' lunch. Enjoy them warm or at room temperature.
These Easy Egg Muffins are a fantastic addition to your kids' lunchbox - a protein-rich and convenient snack that's not only delicious but also customizable with their favorite veggies and cheese. They're a great way to ensure your kids get the energy they need for the day ahead!

Hummus snack packs

Ingredients:

For the Hummus:
1 can (15 oz) chickpeas, drained and rinsed
1/4 cup tahini
1/4 cup fresh lemon juice
1 garlic clove, minced
2 tablespoons olive oil
1/2 teaspoon ground cumin
Salt to taste
Water (as needed for desired consistency)

For the Snack Packs:
Baby carrots
Sliced cucumbers
Bell pepper strips
Cherry tomatoes
Whole-grain pita bread or pretzel crisps

Instructions:

Prepare the Hummus:
In a food processor, combine the chickpeas, tahini, fresh lemon juice, minced garlic, olive oil, ground cumin, and a pinch of salt. Blend until smooth. If the hummus is too thick, add a tablespoon of water at a time until you achieve the desired consistency. Taste and adjust seasoning as needed.

Pack the Snack Packs:
Using small reusable containers or silicone muffin cups, portion out the hummus. In separate compartments of the lunchbox, pack baby carrots, sliced cucumbers, bell pepper strips, cherry tomatoes, and whole-grain pita bread or pretzel crisps.
Encourage your kids to dip the veggies and pita bread into the hummus for a tasty and nutritious snack. The variety of textures and flavors will keep their taste buds happy.

Seal and Keep Cool:
Seal the containers and lunchbox, and keep them cool in the refrigerator until it's time to enjoy.
When it's lunchtime, your kids will have a blast assembling their own hummus snack packs. It's a hands-on, interactive way to enjoy a nutritious and delicious snack.
These Hummus Snack Packs are not only wholesome but also offer a satisfying combination of flavors and textures. They're a great way to encourage kids to eat their veggies and enjoy a protein-packed dip.
These Hummus Snack Packs are a convenient and nutritious addition to your kids' lunchbox - a playful way to enjoy a tasty dip with an assortment of crunchy veggies and whole-grain pita bread. They'll be excited to dip and munch their way through lunchtime!

Coronation chickpea sandwich filler

For the Chickpea Filling:

1 can (15 oz) chickpeas, drained and rinsed
1/4 cup plain Greek yogurt
2 tablespoons mango chutney
1 teaspoon curry powder
1/4 cup diced cucumber
1/4 cup diced red bell pepper
2 tablespoons raisins or dried cranberries
Salt and pepper to taste

For Assembling Sandwiches:

Whole-grain bread slices
Lettuce leaves
Sliced cucumber and bell pepper (optional)

Instructions:

Prepare the Chickpea Filling:
In a mixing bowl, mash the chickpeas with a fork or potato masher until they are partially mashed but still have some texture. Add the Greek yogurt, mango chutney, curry powder, diced cucumber, diced red bell pepper, raisins or dried cranberries, salt, and pepper. Mix well to combine.
Lay out the whole-grain bread slices. Spread a generous layer of the coronation chickpea filling on one slice. Top the chickpea filling with lettuce leaves, sliced cucumber, and bell pepper if desired.
Create the Sandwich:
Place another bread slice on top to create a sandwich.
Cut the sandwich into halves or quarters to fit the lunchbox. Pack the sandwich in a container or wrap it in parchment paper.
Seal and Keep Cool:
Seal the container or wrap securely and keep the lunchbox cool in the refrigerator until lunchtime.
When it's time for lunch, your kids will be excited to open their lunchbox and find a flavorful and unique sandwich waiting for them.
This Coronation Chickpea Sandwich Filler offers a tasty twist on a classic sandwich, providing a blend of sweet, savory, and spicy flavors that's both satisfying and nutritious.
This Coronation Chickpea Sandwich Filler is a delightful addition to your kids' lunchbox - a playful and flavorful alternative to traditional sandwich fillings. With the goodness of chickpeas and the exotic flavors of curry and chutney, it's a lunchtime favorite waiting to be enjoyed!

Fruity skewers with yogurt dip

Ingredients:

For the Fruity Skewers:
Assorted fruits (such as strawberries, grapes, melon, pineapple, and apple)
Wooden skewers (child-safe, if possible)

For the Yogurt Dip:

1/2 cup plain Greek yogurt
1 tablespoon honey (adjust to taste)
1/2 teaspoon vanilla extract (optional)

Instructions:

Prepare the Fruits:
Wash, peel (if needed), and cut the fruits into bite-sized pieces. Keep in mind the size of the skewers and the lunchbox compartments.
Assemble the Skewers:
Thread the fruit pieces onto the wooden skewers in a colorful pattern. You can make them as uniform or as varied as you like.
In a small bowl, mix together the plain Greek yogurt, honey, and vanilla extract (if using). Adjust the sweetness to your liking.
Pack the fruit skewers in a container, making sure to secure the ends of the skewers to prevent any mishaps. Place the yogurt dip in a separate small container.
Seal the containers and the lunchbox, and keep them cool in the refrigerator until lunchtime.
When it's lunchtime, your kids will enjoy the interactive experience of dipping the fruit skewers into the creamy yogurt dip.
These Fruity Skewers with Yogurt Dip are not only visually appealing but also a delightful way to encourage kids to enjoy a variety of fruits and a protein-rich dip.
These Fruity Skewers with Yogurt Dip are a playful and nutritious addition to your kids' lunchbox - a combination of vibrant fruits and a creamy dip that's sure to bring smiles to their faces. It's a snack that's as fun to eat as it is delicious!

Cheesy black bean quesadillas

Ingredients:

For the Quesadillas:
4 whole wheat or spinach tortilla wraps
1 cup black beans, drained and rinsed
1 cup shredded cheddar cheese
1/2 cup diced bell peppers (any color)
1/4 cup diced red onion (optional)
1/4 teaspoon ground cumin
Salt and pepper to taste

For Dipping (Optional):

Salsa or plain Greek yogurt

Instructions:

Prepare the Quesadilla Filling:
In a mixing bowl, combine the black beans, shredded cheddar cheese, diced bell peppers, diced red onion (if using), ground cumin, salt, and pepper. Mix well to combine the flavors.
Assemble the Quesadillas:
Lay out the tortilla wraps on a clean surface. On one half of each wrap, spoon the black bean and cheese mixture. Fold the other half of the wrap over the filling to create a half-moon shape.
Cook the Quesadillas:
Heat a non-stick skillet or griddle over medium heat. Place a folded quesadilla on the skillet and cook for about 2-3 minutes on each side, or until the tortilla is golden brown and the cheese is melted.
Once cooked, remove the quesadillas from the skillet and let them cool for a few minutes. Then, cut each quesadilla into halves or quarters for easy packing.
Pack the cooled quesadilla pieces in the lunchbox compartments. You can also include a small container of salsa or plain Greek yogurt for dipping.
Seal the lunchbox and keep it cool in the refrigerator until it's time for lunch.
When lunchtime arrives, your kids will be excited to enjoy their cheesy black bean quesadillas.
These Cheesy Black Bean Quesadillas are not only scrumptious but also a great source of protein and fiber. They're perfect for satisfying growing appetites and keeping your kids energized.
These Cheesy Black Bean Quesadillas are a delicious and kid-friendly addition to the lunchbox - a warm and cheesy treat that's perfect for little hands to hold and enjoy. With the option of adding salsa or yogurt for dipping, it's a lunchbox favorite waiting to be devoured!

Caprese sandwich

Ingredients:

4 slices whole-grain bread
1 large tomato, thinly sliced
4-6 fresh mozzarella slices
Fresh basil leaves
Balsamic glaze (store-bought or homemade*)
Salt and pepper to taste

Instructions:

Assemble the Sandwich:
Lay out the slices of whole-grain bread. On two slices, arrange the tomato slices, fresh mozzarella slices, and fresh basil leaves. Sprinkle a pinch of salt and pepper over the ingredients.
Drizzle with Balsamic Glaze:
Drizzle a small amount of balsamic glaze over the tomato, mozzarella, and basil. The glaze adds a tangy and sweet flavor that complements the sandwich.
Create the Sandwich:
Place the remaining two slices of bread on top of the tomato, mozzarella, and basil to complete the sandwiches.
Cut the sandwiches in halves or quarters to fit the lunchbox. If desired, wrap each sandwich portion in parchment paper to keep them secure.
Seal the lunchbox and keep it cool in the refrigerator until lunchtime.
When it's time for lunch, your kids will find a fresh and flavorful Caprese sandwich waiting for them.
This Caprese Sandwich is a simple yet elegant option for the lunchbox - a combination of ripe tomatoes, creamy mozzarella, and fragrant basil that's as delicious as it is beautiful.
In a small saucepan, bring 1/2 cup balsamic vinegar to a gentle boil over medium heat. Reduce the heat to low and let it simmer for about 10-15 minutes, or until it has thickened and reduced by half. Let it cool before using. The glaze will continue to thicken as it cools.
This Caprese Sandwich is a delightful and nutritious addition to your kids' lunchbox - a taste of Italy's classic flavors that's perfect for bringing a touch of sophistication to their midday meal.

Spinach savoury muffins

Ingredients:

1 cup all-purpose flour
1 cup whole wheat flour
1 tablespoon baking powder
1/2 teaspoon salt
1/4 teaspoon black pepper
1/2 cup unsalted butter, melted and cooled
1 cup milk
2 large eggs
1 cup fresh spinach, finely chopped
1/2 cup shredded cheddar cheese
1/4 cup grated Parmesan cheese

Instructions:

Preheat the Oven:
Preheat your oven to 375°F (190°C). Line a muffin tin with paper liners or lightly grease the muffin cups.
Mix Dry Ingredients:
In a large mixing bowl, whisk together the all-purpose flour, whole wheat flour, baking powder, salt, and black pepper.
In another bowl, whisk together the melted butter, milk, and eggs until well combined.
Combine Wet and Dry:
Pour the wet ingredients into the dry ingredients and gently stir until just combined. Be cautious not to overmix; a few lumps are okay.
Add Spinach and Cheese:
Fold in the finely chopped fresh spinach, shredded cheddar cheese, and grated Parmesan cheese.
Fill the Muffin Cups:
Using a spoon or ice cream scoop, divide the batter evenly among the muffin cups, filling each about 2/3 full.
Bake the Muffins:
Place the muffin tin in the preheated oven and bake for about 18-20 minutes, or until a toothpick inserted into the center of a muffin comes out clean.
Once baked, remove the muffins from the oven and let them cool in the muffin tin for a few minutes. Then, transfer them to a wire rack to cool completely before packing
Pack the cooled spinach savory muffins in the lunchbox compartments.
Seal the lunchbox and keep it cool in the refrigerator until lunchtime.
When it's lunchtime, your kids will enjoy these flavorful and nutritious spinach savory muffins.
These Spinach Savory Muffins are a wonderful addition to your kids' lunchbox - a tasty and portable way to sneak in some veggies while keeping them satisfied throughout the day.
These Spinach Savory Muffins are not only delicious but also packed with nutrients from the fresh spinach and cheese. They provide a satisfying and wholesome lunchbox option that your kids will eagerly look forward to enjoying.

Chickpea fritters

Ingredients:

For the Chickpea Fritters:
1 can (15 oz) chickpeas, drained and rinsed
1/4 cup finely chopped onion
1/4 cup chopped fresh parsley
1/4 teaspoon ground cumin
1/4 teaspoon ground coriander
1/4 teaspoon garlic powder
1/4 teaspoon baking powder
Salt and pepper to taste
2 tablespoons all-purpose flour
1-2 tablespoons olive oil (for frying)

For the Dip:
1/2 cup plain Greek yogurt
1 tablespoon lemon juice
1/4 teaspoon dried dill
Salt and pepper to taste

Instructions:

Prepare the Chickpea Fritter Batter:
In a food processor, combine the chickpeas, chopped onion, chopped fresh parsley, ground cumin, ground coriander, garlic powder, baking powder, salt, and pepper. Pulse until the mixture is well combined but still has some texture.
Transfer the chickpea mixture to a bowl. Gradually add the all-purpose flour and mix until the batter comes together. The batter should be thick enough to hold its shape.
Using your hands, shape the batter into small patties or fritters. Place them on a plate or tray lined with parchment paper.
In a non-stick skillet, heat the olive oil over medium heat.
Carefully place the chickpea fritters in the skillet and cook for about 2-3 minutes on each side, or until they are golden brown and crispy.
Once cooked, transfer the fritters to a plate lined with paper towels to drain excess oil. Let them cool for a few minutes.
In a small bowl, whisk together the plain Greek yogurt, lemon juice, dried dill, salt, and pepper to make the dip.
Pack the cooled chickpea fritters in the lunchbox compartments along with a small container of the yogurt dip.
Seal the lunchbox and keep it cool in the refrigerator until lunchtime.
When it's lunchtime, your kids will enjoy dipping the chickpea fritters into the flavorful yogurt dip.
These Chickpea Fritters are a delicious and protein-rich addition to your kids' lunchbox - a savory and satisfying snack that's perfect for little hands to hold and enjoy.
These Chickpea Fritters are a delightful option to introduce legumes to your kids' lunchbox - a crispy and flavorful snack that offers a dose of plant-based protein. Paired with the yogurt dip, they become a fantastic and wholesome lunchtime treat!

Falafel lunchbox

Ingredients:

For the Falafel:
1 can (15 oz) chickpeas, drained and rinsed
1/4 cup chopped fresh parsley
1/4 cup chopped fresh cilantro
1/4 cup finely chopped onion
2 cloves garlic, minced
1 teaspoon ground cumin
1/2 teaspoon ground coriander
1/4 teaspoon baking powder
Salt and pepper to taste
2-3 tablespoons all-purpose flour
Olive oil (for frying)

For the Lunchbox:
Whole-grain pita bread or mini pita pockets
Sliced cucumbers
Sliced bell peppers
Cherry tomatoes
Hummus (store-bought or homemade)

Instructions:

Prepare the Falafel Batter:
In a food processor, combine the chickpeas, chopped fresh parsley, chopped fresh cilantro, chopped onion, minced garlic, ground cumin, ground coriander, baking powder, salt, and pepper. Pulse until the mixture is well combined but still has some texture.
Transfer the chickpea mixture to a bowl. Gradually add 2-3 tablespoons of all-purpose flour and mix until the batter holds together. The batter should be thick enough to shape into patties.
Using your hands, shape the batter into small patties or balls. Place them on a plate or tray lined with parchment paper.
In a skillet, heat olive oil over medium heat.
Carefully place the falafel patties in the skillet and cook for about 2-3 minutes on each side, or until they are golden brown and crispy.
Once cooked, transfer the falafel to a plate lined with paper towels to drain excess oil. Let them cool for a few minutes.
Pack the cooled falafel in the lunchbox compartments. Include whole-grain pita bread or mini pita pockets, sliced cucumbers, sliced bell peppers, cherry tomatoes, and a small container of hummus.
Seal the lunchbox and keep it cool in the refrigerator until lunchtime.
When it's lunchtime, your kids will enjoy assembling their own falafel pockets or sandwiches.
This Falafel Lunchbox offers a delightful combination of flavors and textures - crispy falafel, fresh vegetables, and creamy hummus - that's both nutritious and satisfying.
This Falafel Lunchbox is a wonderful way to introduce your kids to the flavors of Middle Eastern cuisine - a tasty and interactive meal that's not only enjoyable but also nutritious and well-balanced.

Easy kids' omelette

Ingredients:

2 large eggs
2 tablespoons milk
Salt and pepper to taste
2 tablespoons shredded cheddar cheese
2 tablespoons diced cooked ham or turkey (optional)
2 tablespoons diced bell peppers (any color)
2 tablespoons diced tomatoes
1 tablespoon chopped fresh parsley or chives (optional)
1 teaspoon butter or cooking oil

Instructions:

Crack the eggs into a bowl. Add milk, a pinch of salt, and a sprinkle of pepper. Whisk the mixture until well combined.
Prepare the diced cooked ham or turkey, diced bell peppers, diced tomatoes, and any other desired fillings.
Heat a non-stick skillet over medium heat. Add butter or cooking oil and let it melt, coating the pan evenly.
Pour the whisked egg mixture into the skillet. Allow it to cook for a minute or until the edges start to set.
Sprinkle the shredded cheddar cheese, diced ham or turkey (if using), diced bell peppers, and diced tomatoes evenly over one half of the omelette.
Gently lift the other half of the omelette and fold it over the fillings, creating a half-moon shape.
Cook the omelette for an additional 1-2 minutes, or until the cheese is melted and the omelette is cooked through.
Carefully slide the omelette onto a plate and let it cool for a few minutes. Once cooled, slice it into halves or quarters for easy packing.
Pack the sliced omelette pieces in the lunchbox compartments.
Seal the lunchbox and keep it cool in the refrigerator until lunchtime.
When it's lunchtime, your kids will have a delicious omelette waiting for them.

Healthy yoghurt and oat muffins

Ingredients:

1 cup rolled oats
1 cup whole wheat flour
1 tsp baking powder
1/2 tsp baking soda
1/2 tsp salt
1/2 tsp cinnamon
1/2 cup Greek yogurt
1/2 cup milk (you can use any type of milk)
1/4 cup honey or maple syrup
1 large egg
1 tsp vanilla extract
1/2 cup mashed ripe banana (about 1 medium-sized banana)
1/2 cup finely grated carrot
1/4 cup chopped nuts (such as walnuts or almonds), optional

Instructions:

Preheat the Oven: Preheat your oven to 350°F (175°C) and line a muffin tin with paper liners or grease with cooking spray.
Prepare the Dry Ingredients: In a bowl, mix together the rolled oats, whole wheat flour, baking powder, baking soda, salt, and cinnamon. Set aside.
Mix the Wet Ingredients: In another bowl, whisk together the Greek yogurt, milk, honey or maple syrup, egg, and vanilla extract until well combined.
Combine Wet and Dry Ingredients: Gradually add the wet ingredients to the dry ingredients and gently stir until just combined. Be careful not to overmix; a few lumps are okay.
Add Fruits and Nuts: Fold in the mashed banana, grated carrot, and chopped nuts (if using) into the batter.
Fill the Muffin Cups: Using a spoon or ice cream scoop, divide the batter evenly among the muffin cups, filling each about 3/4 full.
Bake: Place the muffin tin in the preheated oven and bake for about 18-20 minutes, or until a toothpick inserted into the center of a muffin comes out clean.
Cool: Once done, remove the muffin tin from the oven and allow the muffins to cool in the tin for a few minutes. Then, transfer the muffins to a wire rack to cool completely.
Pack in the Lunch Box: Once the muffins are completely cool, you can pack them in your kid's lunch box. They can enjoy these nutritious muffins as a snack or part of their lunch.

Rainbow quinoa salad

Ingredients:

For the Salad:
1 cup cooked quinoa, cooled
1/2 cup diced red bell pepper
1/2 cup diced orange bell pepper
1/2 cup diced yellow bell pepper
1/2 cup diced cucumber
1/2 cup grated carrot
1/4 cup chopped fresh parsley or cilantro (whichever your child prefers)
1/4 cup crumbled feta cheese (optional)
1/4 cup chopped nuts or seeds (such as almonds, sunflower seeds, or pumpkin seeds)
1/4 cup dried cranberries or raisins (optional)
Salt and pepper to taste

For the Dressing:

3 tablespoons olive oil
2 tablespoons lemon juice
1 teaspoon honey or maple syrup
1/2 teaspoon Dijon mustard (optional)
Salt and pepper to taste

Instructions:

Prepare Quinoa: Cook the quinoa according to the package instructions. Once cooked, allow it to cool to room temperature.
Chop Veggies: Dice the bell peppers (red, orange, and yellow), cucumber, and grate the carrot. Chop the parsley or cilantro.
Make Dressing: In a small bowl, whisk together the olive oil, lemon juice, honey or maple syrup, Dijon mustard, salt, and pepper to make the dressing.
Assemble Salad: In a large bowl, combine the cooled quinoa, diced bell peppers, cucumber, grated carrot, and chopped herbs.
Add Cheese and Nuts: If using, add the crumbled feta cheese, chopped nuts or seeds, and dried cranberries or raisins to the bowl.
Dress the Salad: Drizzle the dressing over the salad and gently toss everything together until well combined. Make sure the dressing is distributed evenly.
Season: Taste and adjust the seasoning with additional salt, pepper, or lemon juice if needed.
Pack in Lunch Box: Divide the rainbow quinoa salad into individual lunch containers. You can include a fork or spoon for easy eating. Seal the containers and refrigerate until ready to pack.
This Rainbow Quinoa Salad is not only visually appealing with its vibrant colors, but it's also packed with nutrients from the various vegetables and quinoa. The dressing adds a delightful zing to the salad, and the feta cheese, nuts, and dried cranberries provide additional flavor and texture. It's a well-balanced and tasty option for your kid's lunch box!

Beetroot chips

Ingredients:

2 medium-sized beets, washed, peeled, and thinly sliced
1 tablespoon olive oil
1/2 teaspoon salt (adjust to taste)
1/4 teaspoon black pepper
Optional seasonings: garlic powder, paprika, or your kid's favorite herbs

Instructions:

Preheat the Oven: Preheat your oven to 325°F (165°C) and line a baking sheet with parchment paper.
Slice Beets: Use a mandoline slicer or a sharp knife to thinly slice the beets. Try to make the slices as even as possible for consistent baking.
Toss with Oil and Seasonings: In a bowl, toss the beet slices with olive oil, salt, pepper, and any optional seasonings you're using. Make sure the slices are well coated.
Arrange on Baking Sheet: Arrange the seasoned beet slices in a single layer on the prepared baking sheet. Avoid overcrowding to ensure even cooking.
Bake: Place the baking sheet in the preheated oven and bake for about 20-25 minutes, or until the beet slices are crispy and slightly curled at the edges. Keep an eye on them as they can burn quickly towards the end.
Cool: Once the beetroot chips are done, remove them from the oven and let them cool on the baking sheet. They will continue to crisp up as they cool.
Pack in Lunch Box: Once the beetroot chips are completely cool and crispy, carefully transfer them to a snack-sized container or a resealable bag. Seal the container or bag and pack them in your kid's lunch box.
Note: Beetroot chips can be a bit delicate, so handle them gently to avoid breaking them. You can also mix the beetroot chips with other vegetable chips or snacks for variety.
These homemade baked beetroot chips are a colorful and nutritious alternative to store-bought potato chips. They are rich in vitamins, minerals, and antioxidants from the beets and offer a satisfying crunch. Plus, they're a fun and tasty way to introduce your kid to different vegetables. Always consider any allergies or dietary preferences when making snacks for your kid's lunch box.

Zucchini and cauliflower fritters

Ingredients:

1 cup grated zucchini (about 1 medium zucchini)
1 cup grated cauliflower florets (about 1/2 small cauliflower)
1/4 cup grated cheddar cheese
1/4 cup finely chopped onion
2 cloves garlic, minced
2 eggs
1/4 cup whole wheat flour or almond flour (for a gluten-free option)
1/2 teaspoon baking powder
1/2 teaspoon salt (adjust to taste)
1/4 teaspoon black pepper
1/2 teaspoon dried herbs (such as oregano, basil, or thyme)
Olive oil for cooking

Instructions:

Prepare the Vegetables: Grate the zucchini using a box grater and place it in a colander. Sprinkle a little salt over the grated zucchini and let it sit for about 10 minutes. This helps draw out excess moisture. After 10 minutes, squeeze out the excess moisture from the zucchini using your hands.
Grate Cauliflower: Grate the cauliflower florets using a box grater or a food processor. You can also use the stem parts of the cauliflower for grating.
Mix Ingredients: In a large bowl, combine the grated zucchini, grated cauliflower, grated cheddar cheese, finely chopped onion, minced garlic, eggs, whole wheat flour (or almond flour), baking powder, salt, black pepper, and dried herbs. Mix everything well until the mixture is combined.
Heat Oil: Heat a non-stick skillet or frying pan over medium heat. Add a small amount of olive oil to coat the bottom of the pan.
Cook Fritters: Using a spoon, scoop portions of the fritter mixture and place them in the pan. Flatten the scoops slightly with the back of the spoon to form fritter shapes. Cook for about 3-4 minutes on each side, or until the fritters are golden brown and cooked through.
Drain and Cool: Once cooked, remove the fritters from the pan and place them on a plate lined with paper towels to drain any excess oil. Allow them to cool slightly before packing them in the lunchbox.
Pack in Lunch Box: Once the fritters are completely cool, pack them in the lunchbox. You can include a small container of dipping sauce such as yogurt-based ranch dressing or tomato salsa.
These Zucchini and Cauliflower Fritters are a fantastic way to sneak in some veggies into your kid's lunch. They are not only tasty but also full of nutrients. Make sure to cool the fritters completely before packing them to avoid moisture buildup in the lunchbox.

Scrambled egg tacos

Ingredients:

For the Scrambled Eggs:

2 large eggs
2 tablespoons milk
Salt and pepper to taste
1 tablespoon butter or cooking oil

For Assembling Tacos:

4 small tortillas (corn or flour)
Grated cheese (cheddar, Monterey Jack, or your kid's favorite)
Sliced veggies (bell peppers, tomatoes, lettuce, etc.)
Salsa or pico de gallo (optional)
Sour cream or Greek yogurt (optional)

Instructions:

Prepare the Scrambled Eggs: In a bowl, whisk together the eggs, milk, salt, and pepper until well combined.
Cook the Eggs: Heat a non-stick skillet over medium heat and add the butter or oil. Once the butter is melted or the oil is heated, pour in the egg mixture.
Scramble the Eggs: Allow the eggs to cook undisturbed for a few seconds until the edges start to set. Then, using a spatula, gently push and fold the eggs from the edges towards the center. Continue this motion, allowing the uncooked egg to flow to the edges. Cook until the eggs are soft, fluffy, and slightly runny. Remove from heat, as residual heat will continue to cook the eggs.
Assemble the Tacos: Warm the tortillas in a dry skillet or microwave them for a few seconds. Place a portion of scrambled eggs onto each tortilla.
Add Toppings: Sprinkle grated cheese over the eggs while they're still warm, so the cheese melts slightly. Then, add sliced veggies, such as bell peppers, tomatoes, or lettuce.
Optional Extras: You can add a spoonful of salsa or pico de gallo for extra flavor and a touch of freshness. A dollop of sour cream or Greek yogurt can also be added if desired.
Fold and Pack: Fold the tortillas into taco shapes and place them in the lunchbox. You can wrap them in parchment paper or aluminum foil to keep them secure.
These Scrambled Egg Tacos are not only delicious but also quite balanced, with protein from the eggs, fiber from the veggies, and whole grains from the tortillas. They're easy to assemble and can be customized with your child's favorite toppings. Consider any allergies or dietary preferences your child might have while preparing the tacos.

Super healthy tahini balls

Ingredients:

1 cup rolled oats
1/2 cup tahini
1/4 cup honey or maple syrup
1/2 cup ground flaxseeds
1/2 cup shredded coconut
(unsweetened)
1/2 teaspoon vanilla extract
Pinch of salt
Optional add-ins: chocolate chips, chopped nuts, dried fruit, chia seeds

Instructions:

Combine Ingredients: In a large mixing bowl, combine rolled oats, tahini, honey or maple syrup, ground flaxseeds, shredded coconut, vanilla extract, and a pinch of salt. Mix well until the ingredients are evenly combined.
Add Optional Add-ins: If desired, you can add optional add-ins like chocolate chips, chopped nuts, dried fruit, or chia seeds. These additions can provide extra flavor, texture, and nutrients.
Chill the Mixture: Place the mixture in the refrigerator for about 15-20 minutes. Chilling the mixture will make it easier to handle and shape into balls.
Shape into Balls: After chilling, take small portions of the mixture and roll them between your palms to form bite-sized balls. The mixture might be slightly sticky, but it should hold its shape.
Set and Store: Place the tahini balls on a parchment-lined tray or plate and let them set in the refrigerator for another 20-30 minutes. This will help the balls firm up.
Pack in Lunch Box: Once the tahini balls are set, transfer them to an airtight container or snack-sized resealable bags. You can include a few tahini balls in your kid's lunchbox for a nutritious snack.
These Super Healthy Tahini Balls are a great source of energy, healthy fats, fiber, and protein. They can provide a quick boost during busy school days and keep your child satisfied until their next meal. Plus, they are customizable with various add-ins to suit your child's taste preferences. Just make sure to consider any allergies your child might have before adding ingredients.

Coconut rough slice

Ingredients:

For the Base:
1 1/2 cups shredded coconut
1/2 cup almond meal or finely ground almonds
1/4 cup cocoa powder
1/4 cup honey or maple syrup
2 tablespoons coconut oil, melted
1/2 teaspoon vanilla extract
Pinch of salt

For the Chocolate Topping:

1/2 cup dark chocolate chips or chopped dark chocolate
1 tablespoon coconut oil

Instructions:
Prepare the Base:
Line Pan: Line a square or rectangular baking pan with parchment paper, leaving some overhang on the sides for easy removal.
Mix Base Ingredients: In a mixing bowl, combine shredded coconut, almond meal, cocoa powder, honey or maple syrup, melted coconut oil, vanilla extract, and a pinch of salt. Mix well until the mixture is thoroughly combined.
Press into Pan: Press the mixture firmly and evenly into the prepared baking pan, creating an even layer. Use the back of a spoon or your hands to press it down.
Chill: Place the pan in the refrigerator while you prepare the chocolate topping. This will allow the base to firm up a bit.
Melt Chocolate and Coconut Oil: In a microwave-safe bowl or using a double boiler, melt the dark chocolate chips or chopped dark chocolate along with the coconut oil. Stir until smooth and well combined.
Pour Chocolate: Remove the baking pan from the refrigerator. Pour the melted chocolate mixture over the base layer.
Spread Chocolate: Use a spatula to spread the chocolate evenly over the base, covering it completely.
Chill: Place the pan back in the refrigerator to allow the chocolate topping to set. This will take around 1-2 hours.
Slice: Once the chocolate is set, remove the pan from the refrigerator. Use the parchment paper overhangs to lift the entire Coconut Rough Slice out of the pan.
Slice into Bars: Place the slice on a cutting board and use a sharp knife to slice it into small bars or squares.
Pack in Lunch Box: Pack the Coconut Rough Bars into your kid's lunchbox. They can be wrapped in parchment paper or placed in small snack-sized resealable bags.

Red onion and green pea fritters

Ingredients:

1 cup frozen green peas, thawed
1 small red onion, finely chopped
1/2 cup all-purpose flour (or chickpea flour for a gluten-free option)
2 eggs
1/2 teaspoon baking powder
Salt and pepper to taste
Cooking oil (such as vegetable or olive oil)

Instructions:

Prepare the Peas: Thaw the frozen green peas by rinsing them under cold water or leaving them at room temperature for a while. You can also quickly steam them until tender.

Mix Batter: In a mixing bowl, beat the eggs. Add the finely chopped red onion, thawed green peas, all-purpose flour (or chickpea flour), baking powder, salt, and pepper. Mix well until the ingredients are combined and a batter forms.

Adjust Consistency: Depending on the consistency of the batter, you can add a little more flour if it's too runny or a splash of water/milk if it's too thick. The batter should be thick enough to hold its shape but not too dry.

Heat Oil: Heat a non-stick skillet or frying pan over medium heat. Add enough cooking oil to coat the bottom of the pan.

Cook Fritters: Once the oil is hot, spoon portions of the batter onto the skillet to form fritters. Use the back of the spoon to flatten and shape them slightly. Cook for about 2-3 minutes on each side, or until the fritters are golden brown and crispy.

Drain and Cool: Remove the cooked fritters from the skillet and place them on a plate lined with paper towels to drain any excess oil. Allow them to cool slightly.

Pack in Lunch Box: Once the fritters are cool, place them in your kid's lunchbox. You can include a small container of dipping sauce like yogurt-based ranch dressing or ketchup.

These Red Onion and Green Pea Fritters are a creative and flavorful way to incorporate vegetables into your kid's lunch. They offer a balance of protein, fiber, and nutrients from the peas and onions. Ensure that the fritters are cooled completely before packing to avoid condensation in the lunchbox.

Berry carrot loaf

Ingredients:

1 1/2 cups all-purpose flour (or whole wheat flour for a healthier version)
1/2 cup granulated sugar (you can adjust the sweetness according to preference)
1 teaspoon baking powder
1/2 teaspoon baking soda
1/2 teaspoon ground cinnamon
1/4 teaspoon salt
2 large eggs
1/2 cup vegetable oil (or melted coconut oil)
1 teaspoon vanilla extract
1 cup grated carrots
1/2 cup mixed berries (such as blueberries, raspberries, or chopped strawberries)
1/4 cup chopped nuts (optional)
Powdered sugar for dusting (optional)

Instructions:

Preheat Oven: Preheat your oven to 350°F (175°C). Grease and flour a loaf pan or line it with parchment paper for easy removal.
Mix Dry Ingredients: In a large mixing bowl, whisk together the flour, sugar, baking powder, baking soda, ground cinnamon, and salt.
Combine Wet Ingredients: In another bowl, beat the eggs. Add the vegetable oil and vanilla extract, and mix well.
Combine Wet and Dry: Pour the wet ingredients into the dry ingredients and mix until just combined. Do not overmix; a few lumps are okay.
Add Carrots and Berries: Gently fold in the grated carrots and mixed berries into the batter. If using nuts, add them now as well.
Bake: Pour the batter into the prepared loaf pan. Smooth the top with a spatula. Bake in the preheated oven for about 50-60 minutes, or until a toothpick inserted into the center comes out clean.
Cool: Once baked, remove the loaf from the oven and let it cool in the pan for about 10 minutes. Then, transfer it to a wire rack to cool completely.
Slice and Pack: Once the Berry Carrot Loaf is completely cool, slice it into portions suitable for your kid's lunchbox. You can dust the slices with powdered sugar if desired.
Pack in Lunch Box: Place the slices of Berry Carrot Loaf in your kid's lunchbox. You can also include a small container of cream cheese or nut butter for spreading, if your child enjoys that.
This Berry Carrot Loaf is a wonderful combination of fruity sweetness from the berries and natural sweetness from the carrots. It's a great way to sneak in some extra veggies and fruits into your child's diet. Always consider any allergies or dietary preferences your child might have while preparing and packing their lunch.

Sweet Potato Nachos

Ingredients:

2 medium sweet potatoes, washed and sliced into thin rounds
2 tablespoons olive oil
1 teaspoon chili powder
1/2 teaspoon ground cumin
1/2 teaspoon paprika
Salt to taste
1 cup shredded cheddar cheese (or any preferred cheese)
1/2 cup cooked black beans (canned or homemade)
1/4 cup diced tomatoes
1/4 cup diced bell peppers (assorted colors)
1/4 cup diced red onion
1/4 cup sliced black olives
Optional toppings: sour cream, guacamole, salsa

Instructions:

Preheat Oven: Preheat your oven to 400°F (200°C).
Prepare Sweet Potato Rounds: In a large bowl, toss the sweet potato rounds with olive oil, chili powder, ground cumin, paprika, and a pinch of salt. Ensure that the sweet potato slices are coated evenly with the spices.
Arrange and Bake: Arrange the seasoned sweet potato rounds in a single layer on a baking sheet lined with parchment paper. Bake in the preheated oven for about 15-20 minutes, or until the sweet potatoes are crisp and slightly browned.
Add Cheese and Toppings: Remove the baking sheet from the oven and sprinkle the shredded cheese over the sweet potato rounds. Return the baking sheet to the oven and bake for an additional 3-5 minutes, or until the cheese is melted.
Assemble Nachos: Once the cheese is melted and bubbly, remove the baking sheet from the oven. Let the sweet potato nachos cool slightly before carefully transferring them to a lunch container.
Add Toppings: Evenly distribute the cooked black beans, diced tomatoes, diced bell peppers, diced red onion, and sliced black olives over the sweet potato nachos.
Optional Toppings: If your child enjoys them, you can also include small containers of sour cream, guacamole, and salsa for dipping.
Pack in Lunch Box: Pack the assembled Sweet Potato Nachos in your kid's lunchbox. Make sure to include any optional dipping sauces or toppings in separate containers.
These Sweet Potato Nachos are a healthier twist on traditional nachos, with sweet potato slices as the base and nutritious toppings. They provide a balance of flavors and textures that your child will love. As always, consider any allergies or dietary preferences your child might have when preparing their lunch.

Chicken and vegie hummus wrap

Ingredients:

1 large whole wheat or whole grain tortilla wrap
2 tablespoons hummus (choose your kid's favorite flavor)
2-3 slices cooked chicken (grilled or roasted), thinly sliced
1/4 cup shredded lettuce or baby spinach
1/4 cup grated carrots
1/4 cup sliced bell peppers (assorted colors)
1/4 cup cucumber slices
Salt and pepper to taste

Instructions:

Prepare the Wrap: Lay the tortilla wrap flat on a clean surface.
Spread Hummus: Spread a layer of hummus evenly over the surface of the tortilla, leaving a border around the edges.
Layer Ingredients: Place the thinly sliced cooked chicken in a single layer over the hummus.
Add Veggies: Sprinkle the shredded lettuce or baby spinach, grated carrots, sliced bell peppers, and cucumber slices over the chicken.
Season: Season the veggies with a pinch of salt and a sprinkle of black pepper, if desired.
Roll Up: Starting from one end, tightly roll up the tortilla, tucking in the sides as you go to create a neat wrap.
Slice and Pack: Carefully slice the wrap into halves or smaller portions suitable for your kid's lunchbox. If the wrap is not staying closed, you can use a toothpick to hold it in place until lunchtime.
Pack in Lunch Box: Pack the Chicken and Veggie Hummus Wrap portions in your kid's lunchbox. You can include a small container of extra hummus for dipping if they like.
This Chicken and Veggie Hummus Wrap is not only tasty but also provides a balanced combination of protein, fiber, and nutrients from the chicken, hummus, and colorful veggies. It's a great option to keep your kid fueled and satisfied throughout the day. Remember to consider any allergies or dietary preferences your child might have while preparing their lunch.

Crispy air fryer Italian frittole

Ingredients:

1 cup all-purpose flour
1 teaspoon baking powder
1/4 teaspoon salt
1/2 cup milk
1 large egg
1/4 cup grated Parmesan cheese
1/4 cup finely chopped fresh herbs (such as parsley, basil, or oregano)
1/4 cup cooked and finely chopped vegetables (such as zucchini, bell peppers, or corn)
Cooking oil spray
Marinara sauce or tomato sauce for dipping

Instructions:

Preheat Air Fryer: Preheat your air fryer to 350°F (175°C) for a few minutes.
Mix Dry Ingredients: In a mixing bowl, whisk together the all-purpose flour, baking powder, and salt.
Prepare Batter: In a separate bowl, whisk together the milk and egg until well combined.
Combine Wet and Dry: Gradually add the wet ingredients to the dry ingredients, whisking until a smooth batter forms.
Add Cheese and Herbs: Stir in the grated Parmesan cheese and finely chopped fresh herbs into the batter.
Add Chopped Vegetables: Gently fold in the cooked and finely chopped vegetables of your choice.
Shape Frittole: Lightly grease the air fryer basket or tray with cooking oil spray. Using a spoon, drop spoonfuls of the batter into the air fryer, leaving some space between them.
Air Fry: Place the frittole in the preheated air fryer and cook at 350°F (175°C) for about 8-10 minutes, or until they are golden brown and crispy on the outside. You may need to cook them in batches, depending on the size of your air fryer.
Cool and Pack: Once the frittole are cooked, remove them from the air fryer and let them cool slightly. Then, pack them in your kid's lunchbox.
Add Dipping Sauce: Include a small container of marinara sauce or tomato sauce for dipping.
These Crispy Air Fryer Italian Frittole are a wonderful twist on the traditional frittole with added herbs and vegetables. They provide a satisfying and flavorful snack that's easy to make and perfect for a kid's lunchbox. As always, consider any allergies or dietary preferences your child might have while preparing the recipe.

Cheesy cauliflower spelt muffins

Ingredients:

1 cup spelt flour (or whole wheat flour for a similar nutty flavor)
1 teaspoon baking powder
1/2 teaspoon baking soda
1/2 teaspoon salt
1/4 teaspoon black pepper
1/2 cup finely grated cauliflower (blanched and drained)
1 cup grated cheddar cheese
1/4 cup finely chopped fresh herbs (such as parsley, chives, or thyme)
1/2 cup milk (any type of milk)
1/4 cup plain Greek yogurt
1/4 cup olive oil or melted butter
1 large egg

Instructions:

Preheat Oven: Preheat your oven to 375°F (190°C). Line a muffin tin with paper liners or grease the muffin cups.
Mix Dry Ingredients: In a mixing bowl, whisk together the spelt flour, baking powder, baking soda, salt, and black pepper.
Prepare Cauliflower: Finely grate the cauliflower using a grater or food processor. Blanche the grated cauliflower in boiling water for about 2 minutes, then drain well and pat dry with a clean towel to remove excess moisture.
Combine Wet Ingredients: In another bowl, whisk together the milk, Greek yogurt, olive oil or melted butter, and the egg until well combined.
Combine Wet and Dry: Gradually add the wet ingredients to the dry ingredients and gently mix until just combined. Be careful not to overmix; a few lumps are okay.
Add Cauliflower, Cheese, and Herbs: Fold in the finely grated cauliflower, grated cheddar cheese, and chopped fresh herbs into the batter.
Fill Muffin Cups: Divide the batter evenly among the muffin cups, filling each about 3/4 full.
Bake: Place the muffin tin in the preheated oven and bake for about 18-20 minutes, or until the muffins are golden brown and a toothpick inserted into the center comes out clean.
Cool and Pack: Once done, remove the muffin tin from the oven and allow the muffins to cool in the tin for a few minutes. Then, transfer the muffins to a wire rack to cool completely before packing them in your kid's lunchbox.
Pack in Lunch Box: Once the Cheesy Cauliflower Spelt Muffins are completely cool, pack them in your kid's lunchbox. They can enjoy these savory and nutritious muffins as a snack or part of their lunch.
These Cheesy Cauliflower Spelt Muffins are a fantastic way to sneak in some veggies while also offering the delightful taste of cheese and herbs. They make for a wholesome and tasty addition to your child's lunchbox. Remember to consider any allergies or dietary preferences your child might have while preparing the recipe.

Easy spinach and ricotta muffins

Ingredients:

1 cup all-purpose flour
1 teaspoon baking powder
1/2 teaspoon baking soda
1/2 teaspoon salt
1/4 teaspoon black pepper
1/2 cup fresh baby spinach, finely chopped
1/2 cup ricotta cheese
1/4 cup grated Parmesan cheese
1/4 cup milk
1/4 cup olive oil
1 large egg

Instructions:

Preheat Oven: Preheat your oven to 375°F (190°C). Line a muffin tin with paper liners or grease the muffin cups.
Mix Dry Ingredients: In a mixing bowl, whisk together the all-purpose flour, baking powder, baking soda, salt, and black pepper.
Prepare Spinach: Finely chop the fresh baby spinach. You can use a food processor for this step.
Combine Wet Ingredients: In another bowl, whisk together the ricotta cheese, grated Parmesan cheese, milk, olive oil, and the egg until well combined.
Combine Wet and Dry: Gradually add the wet ingredients to the dry ingredients and gently mix until just combined. Do not overmix; a few lumps are okay.
Add Spinach: Gently fold in the finely chopped baby spinach into the batter.
Fill Muffin Cups: Divide the batter evenly among the muffin cups, filling each about 3/4 full.
Bake: Place the muffin tin in the preheated oven and bake for about 18-20 minutes, or until the muffins are golden brown and a toothpick inserted into the center comes out clean.
Cool and Pack: Once done, remove the muffin tin from the oven and allow the muffins to cool in the tin for a few minutes. Then, transfer the muffins to a wire rack to cool completely before packing them in your kid's lunchbox.
Pack in Lunch Box: Once the Easy Spinach and Ricotta Muffins are completely cool, pack them in your kid's lunchbox. These muffins offer a savory and nutritious option for a snack or a meal on-the-go.
These Easy Spinach and Ricotta Muffins are a great way to incorporate greens and dairy into your child's diet. They are easy to prepare and make for a flavorful and wholesome addition to their lunch. Remember to consider any allergies or dietary preferences your child might have while preparing the recipe.

Bagel pizzas

Ingredients:

2 plain or whole wheat bagels, sliced in half
1/2 cup pizza sauce or marinara sauce
1 cup shredded mozzarella cheese
Toppings of choice: sliced pepperoni, diced bell peppers, sliced olives, cooked and crumbled sausage, diced tomatoes, etc.
Italian seasoning or dried oregano (optional)

Instructions:

Preheat Oven: Preheat your oven to 375°F (190°C).
Prepare Bagel Halves: Lay the bagel halves on a baking sheet or oven-safe tray, cut side up.
Add Sauce: Spread a tablespoon of pizza sauce or marinara sauce over each bagel half.
Sprinkle Cheese: Sprinkle a generous amount of shredded mozzarella cheese over the sauce on each bagel half.
Add Toppings: Add your chosen toppings over the cheese. Get creative and involve your kid in choosing their favorite toppings.
Season: If desired, sprinkle a pinch of Italian seasoning or dried oregano over the toppings for extra flavor.
Bake: Place the baking sheet with the prepared bagel pizzas in the preheated oven. Bake for about 10-12 minutes, or until the cheese is melted and bubbly, and the edges of the bagels are golden brown.
Cool and Pack: Once the bagel pizzas are cooked, remove them from the oven and let them cool slightly. Then, pack them in your kid's lunchbox.
Pack in Lunch Box: Once the Bagel Pizzas are completely cool, pack them in your kid's lunchbox. They can enjoy these mini pizzas as a tasty and satisfying lunchtime treat.
Bagel Pizzas are a fun way to enjoy the flavors of pizza in a convenient and handheld form. They offer a great opportunity to customize flavors and include a variety of toppings. As always, consider any allergies or dietary preferences your child might have while preparing the recipe.

Mini bread quiches

Ingredients:

6 slices of whole wheat bread (or bread of choice)
1/2 cup cooked and finely chopped vegetables (spinach, bell peppers, broccoli, etc.)
1/2 cup shredded cheddar cheese (or cheese of choice)
3 large eggs
1/2 cup milk (any type of milk)
Salt and pepper to taste
Cooking oil spray

Instructions:

Preheat Oven: Preheat your oven to 375°F (190°C). Grease a muffin tin or line it with paper liners.
Prepare Bread: Flatten each slice of bread with a rolling pin to thin it out slightly. Press the flattened bread slices into the muffin cups to create a cup shape. The bread will form the crust for the mini quiches.
Add Vegetables and Cheese: Divide the chopped vegetables and shredded cheese among the bread cups.
Prepare Egg Mixture: In a bowl, whisk together the eggs, milk, salt, and pepper until well combined.
Pour Egg Mixture: Carefully pour the egg mixture into each bread cup, filling them almost to the top.
Bake: Place the muffin tin in the preheated oven and bake for about 15-20 minutes, or until the egg is set and the tops are golden brown.
Cool and Pack: Once the mini bread quiches are done, remove them from the oven and let them cool slightly. Then, remove them from the muffin tin and pack them in your kid's lunchbox.
Pack in Lunch Box: Once the Mini Bread Quiches are completely cool, pack them in your kid's lunchbox. These mini quiches make for a delicious and nutritious lunch or snack option.
These Mini Bread Quiches are a great way to include veggies and protein in your child's lunch. They're convenient and offer a wonderful blend of flavors. Customize the fillings based on your child's preferences and any dietary considerations.

Cucumber sushi

Ingredients:

1 large cucumber
1 cup sushi rice, cooked and seasoned with rice vinegar, sugar, and salt
Sliced vegetables of choice (carrots, bell peppers, avocado, etc.)
Cooked protein of choice (cooked shrimp, imitation crab, cooked chicken, etc.)
Soy sauce or tamari for dipping (optional)

Instructions:

Prepare Cucumber: Wash and peel the cucumber. Cut it into thin strips using a vegetable peeler, mandoline slicer, or knife. Lay the cucumber slices on paper towels to remove excess moisture.
Lay Out Ingredients: Prepare all your ingredients—sushi rice, sliced vegetables, and cooked protein—so they're ready for assembly.
Assemble Sushi Rolls: Lay a cucumber slice flat and place a small amount of sushi rice on one end. Add a few slices of vegetables and a piece of cooked protein.
Roll: Carefully roll up the cucumber slice, starting from the end with the rice and fillings. The cucumber slice should naturally adhere to itself.
Secure: If needed, you can secure the end of the roll with a toothpick, but make sure to inform your child about it if you do.
Repeat: Repeat the process with the remaining cucumber slices and fillings.
Pack in Lunch Box: Place the assembled cucumber sushi rolls in your kid's lunchbox. You can include a small container of soy sauce or tamari for dipping, if desired.
Tips:
You can get creative with the fillings based on your child's preferences. Make sure to slice the vegetables and protein thinly for easy rolling.
If your child is a fan of nori (seaweed), you can also wrap a thin strip of nori around the cucumber roll to mimic the traditional sushi look.
To prevent the cucumber rolls from getting soggy, you can place a piece of parchment paper between layers in the lunchbox.
Cucumber sushi rolls offer a refreshing and crunchy twist on traditional sushi, making them a delightful and nutritious lunchbox option. Consider any allergies or dietary preferences your child might have while preparing the recipe.

Smashed chickpea and vegie wrap

Ingredients:

1 small can (15 oz) chickpeas, drained and rinsed
1/4 cup diced red bell pepper
1/4 cup diced cucumber
1/4 cup finely chopped carrot
2 tablespoons finely chopped fresh herbs (such as parsley or cilantro)
2 tablespoons Greek yogurt or mayo (adjust quantity based on preference)
1 teaspoon lemon juice
Salt and pepper to taste
2 large whole wheat or spinach tortilla wraps
Leafy greens (lettuce, spinach, etc.)

Instructions:

Prepare Chickpea Mixture: In a bowl, mash the chickpeas using a fork or potato masher until they're roughly smashed. You can leave some chunks for texture.
Add Veggies and Herbs: To the mashed chickpeas, add the diced red bell pepper, diced cucumber, finely chopped carrot, and chopped fresh herbs. Mix well.
Add Greek Yogurt/Mayo: Stir in the Greek yogurt or mayo to bind the mixture together. Adjust the quantity based on how creamy you'd like the filling.
Season: Add the lemon juice, salt, and pepper to taste. Mix everything until well combined.
Assemble Wraps: Lay out the tortilla wraps and place a layer of leafy greens in the center of each wrap.
Add Chickpea Mixture: Divide the smashed chickpea and veggie mixture between the two wraps, placing it on top of the greens.
Add Optional Ingredients: If desired, you can add some shredded cheese and sliced avocado on top of the chickpea mixture.
Roll Up: Carefully fold in the sides of the wraps and then roll them up tightly, enclosing the filling.
Slice and Pack: Slice the wraps in half diagonally or leave them whole, depending on your child's preference. Pack them in your kid's lunchbox.
Pack in Lunch Box: Once the Smashed Chickpea and Veggie Wraps are prepared, pack them in your kid's lunchbox. These wraps offer a delicious and protein-packed option for lunch or snack time.
This Smashed Chickpea and Veggie Wrap is not only flavorful but also packed with nutrients from the chickpeas and various vegetables. Feel free to customize the ingredients based on your child's taste preferences. Always consider any allergies or dietary preferences your child might have while preparing their lunch.

Ham, avocado and cheese wraps

Ingredients:

2 large whole wheat or spinach tortilla wraps
4-6 slices of cooked ham
1 ripe avocado, sliced
1/2 cup shredded cheddar cheese (or cheese of choice)
Leafy greens (lettuce, spinach, etc.)
Mustard or mayonnaise (optional)
Salt and pepper to taste

Instructions:

Prepare Wraps: Lay out the tortilla wraps on a clean surface.
Layer Ingredients: Place 2-3 slices of cooked ham on each wrap, spreading them out evenly.
Add Avocado Slices: Lay avocado slices over the ham on each wrap.
Sprinkle Cheese: Sprinkle shredded cheddar cheese over the avocado.
Add Leafy Greens: Place a layer of leafy greens, such as lettuce or spinach, on top of the cheese.
Add Condiments: If desired, add a thin layer of mustard or mayonnaise on the greens for added flavor.
Season: Sprinkle a pinch of salt and pepper over the ingredients.
Roll Up: Carefully fold in the sides of the wraps and then roll them up tightly, enclosing the filling.
Slice and Pack: Slice the wraps in half diagonally or leave them whole, depending on your child's preference. Pack them in your kid's lunchbox.
Pack in Lunch Box: Once the Ham, Avocado, and Cheese Wraps are prepared, pack them in your kid's lunchbox. These wraps offer a balanced combination of protein, healthy fats, and greens.
These Ham, Avocado, and Cheese Wraps are not only tasty but also provide a satisfying and nutritious lunch option. Customize the ingredients and condiments based on your child's taste preferences. Always consider any allergies or dietary preferences your child might have while preparing their lunch.

Cheese and mustard soft pretzels

Ingredients:

For the Pretzel Dough:
2 1/4 teaspoons active dry yeast
1 cup warm water (about 110°F/43°C)
1 tablespoon granulated sugar
3 cups all-purpose flour
1 teaspoon salt

For the Topping:

1/4 cup mustard (Dijon or your favorite mustard)
1/2 cup grated cheddar cheese (or cheese of choice)
Coarse sea salt

Instructions:

Prepare the Dough: In a bowl, dissolve the sugar in warm water and sprinkle the yeast over it. Allow the yeast to activate for about 5-10 minutes until it becomes frothy.
Mix Dough: In a larger mixing bowl, combine the flour and salt. Add the activated yeast mixture and mix until a dough forms.
Knead Dough: Turn the dough onto a lightly floured surface and knead for about 5-7 minutes, until the dough is smooth and elastic.
Rise: Place the dough in a greased bowl, cover it with a clean kitchen towel, and let it rise in a warm place for about 1 hour, or until doubled in size.
Preheat Oven: Preheat your oven to 425°F (220°C). Line a baking sheet with parchment paper.
Shape Pretzels: Punch down the risen dough and divide it into equal portions. Roll each portion into a long rope. Shape the ropes into pretzels by making a U-shape, then cross the ends and press them onto the curved part of the U.
Boil Pretzels: Bring a large pot of water to a boil. Carefully add the pretzels, one or two at a time, and boil for about 30 seconds. Remove them using a slotted spoon and place them on a paper towel to drain excess water.
Topping: Place the boiled pretzels on the prepared baking sheet. Brush each pretzel with mustard and sprinkle with grated cheese. Lightly sprinkle coarse sea salt over the tops.
Bake: Bake in the preheated oven for about 12-15 minutes, or until the pretzels are golden brown and the cheese is melted.
Cool and Pack: Allow the Cheese and Mustard Soft Pretzels to cool slightly before packing them in your kid's lunchbox.
Pack in Lunch Box: Once the pretzels are completely cool, pack them in your kid's lunchbox. These pretzels offer a unique twist on the classic pretzel, with a cheesy and tangy mustard topping.
These Cheese and Mustard Soft Pretzels are a flavorful and satisfying snack or lunch option. Remember to consider any allergies or dietary preferences your child might have while preparing the recipe.

Chicken sausage rolls

Ingredients:

For the Filling:

1 cup ground chicken (cooked and seasoned)
1/2 cup finely chopped vegetables (carrots, bell peppers, zucchini, etc.)
1/4 cup breadcrumbs
1/4 cup grated cheese (cheddar or mozzarella)
1 teaspoon dried herbs (such as thyme or oregano)
Salt and pepper to taste

For the Pastry:

1 sheet puff pastry (thawed if frozen)
1 egg (beaten, for egg wash)

Instructions:

Preheat Oven: Preheat your oven to 375°F (190°C). Line a baking sheet with parchment paper.
Prepare Filling: In a bowl, combine the cooked and seasoned ground chicken, finely chopped vegetables, breadcrumbs, grated cheese, dried herbs, salt, and pepper. Mix well until everything is evenly distributed.
Roll Out Pastry: Roll out the puff pastry sheet on a lightly floured surface to a rectangle. Cut the pastry sheet in half lengthwise.
Add Filling: Divide the chicken and vegetable filling into two portions. Place each portion of filling in the center of each pastry half, shaping it into a log along the length.
Roll Up: Carefully roll up the pastry around the filling, sealing the edges with a little water to help them stick.
Cut and Seal: Cut each rolled-up log into smaller portions, about 2 inches in length. Use a fork to press down and seal the edges of each portion.
Brush with Egg Wash: Place the sausage rolls on the prepared baking sheet. Brush the tops with beaten egg for a golden finish when baked.
Bake: Bake in the preheated oven for about 20-25 minutes, or until the sausage rolls are puffed up and golden brown.
Cool and Pack: Allow the Chicken Sausage Rolls to cool slightly before packing them in your kid's lunchbox.
Pack in Lunch Box: Once the sausage rolls are completely cool, pack them in your kid's lunchbox. These sausage rolls are a savory and protein-packed option for lunch or snack time.
These Chicken Sausage Rolls are a kid-friendly version of the classic sausage roll, made with chicken and flavorful vegetables. As always, consider any allergies or dietary preferences your child might have while preparing their lunch.

Summer salad sandwich

Ingredients:

4 slices of whole wheat bread (or bread of choice)
1/2 cup cooked and diced chicken or turkey (optional)
1/2 cup diced cucumber
1/2 cup diced ripe tomatoes
1/4 cup diced red bell pepper
1/4 cup diced red onion
1/4 cup diced avocado
1/4 cup shredded lettuce or spinach
2 tablespoons mayonnaise or Greek yogurt
1 teaspoon Dijon mustard (optional)
Salt and pepper to taste

Instructions:

Prepare Ingredients: In a bowl, combine the cooked and diced chicken or turkey (if using), diced cucumber, diced tomatoes, diced red bell pepper, diced red onion, diced avocado, and shredded lettuce or spinach.
Add Dressing: Add mayonnaise or Greek yogurt to the bowl. If desired, add Dijon mustard for extra flavor. Mix everything well until the ingredients are coated in the dressing.
Season: Season the mixture with salt and pepper to taste. Adjust the seasoning according to your child's preference.
Assemble Sandwiches: Lay out the slices of bread. Divide the salad mixture evenly and place it on two slices of bread.
Create Sandwiches: Top the salad mixture with the remaining two slices of bread to create two sandwiches.
Slice and Pack: If desired, slice the sandwiches in halves or quarters to fit the lunchbox. Pack the Summer Salad Sandwiches in your kid's lunchbox.
Pack in Lunch Box: Once the sandwiches are prepared, pack them in your kid's lunchbox. These sandwiches offer a refreshing and nutritious option for a summer-inspired lunch.
The Summer Salad Sandwich is a light and flavorful alternative to traditional sandwiches, perfect for warm weather. Customize the ingredients based on your child's taste preferences and any dietary considerations. Always consider any allergies your child might have while preparing their lunch.

Ham and egg wrap

Ingredients:

1 large whole wheat or spinach tortilla wrap
2 large eggs
2 slices of cooked ham
1/4 cup shredded cheddar cheese (or cheese of choice)
Salt and pepper to taste
Optional toppings: diced tomatoes, chopped spinach, salsa, etc.

Instructions:

Prepare Eggs: In a bowl, whisk the eggs together until well beaten. Season with a pinch of salt and pepper.
Cook Eggs: Heat a non-stick skillet over medium heat. Pour the beaten eggs into the skillet and cook, stirring gently, until they are scrambled and cooked to your desired consistency. Remove from heat.
Warm Tortilla: Warm the tortilla wrap in the microwave for a few seconds until it's pliable.
Assemble Wrap: Lay the warmed tortilla on a clean surface. Place the slices of cooked ham in the center of the tortilla.
Add Eggs and Cheese: Spoon the scrambled eggs on top of the ham. Sprinkle the shredded cheddar cheese over the eggs.
Add Toppings: If desired, add optional toppings like diced tomatoes or chopped spinach.
Roll Up: Fold in the sides of the tortilla and then tightly roll it up from the bottom to enclose the filling.
Slice and Pack: If desired, slice the wrap in half diagonally for easier eating. Pack the Ham and Egg Wrap in your kid's lunchbox.
Pack in Lunch Box: Once the Ham and Egg Wrap is prepared, pack it in your kid's lunchbox. This wrap offers a protein-rich and satisfying option for lunch or snack time.
The Ham and Egg Wrap is a classic and versatile option that's easy to make and customize based on your child's preferences. Remember to consider any allergies or dietary preferences your child might have while preparing their lunch.

Salmon and potato salad

Ingredients:

For the Salad:
1 cup cooked and flaked salmon (canned or cooked fresh)
1 1/2 cups cooked and diced potatoes (you can use leftover boiled potatoes)
1/2 cup diced cucumber
1/4 cup diced red onion
1/4 cup diced bell peppers (any color)
1/4 cup chopped fresh dill (or herb of choice)
1/4 cup chopped fresh parsley
Salt and pepper to taste

For the Dressing:

2 tablespoons mayonnaise or Greek yogurt
1 tablespoon lemon juice
1 teaspoon Dijon mustard (optional)
Salt and pepper to taste

Instructions:

Prepare Ingredients: In a large bowl, combine the cooked and flaked salmon, diced potatoes, diced cucumber, diced red onion, diced bell peppers, chopped dill, and chopped parsley.

Make Dressing: In a small bowl, whisk together the mayonnaise or Greek yogurt, lemon juice, Dijon mustard (if using), salt, and pepper until well combined.

Add Dressing: Pour the dressing over the salmon and potato mixture. Gently toss everything to coat the ingredients with the dressing.

Season: Taste the salad and adjust the salt and pepper according to your preference.

Pack in Lunch Box: Pack the Salmon and Potato Salad in your kid's lunchbox. You can use a separate container to keep the salad fresh.

Rhubarb bran muffins

Ingredients:

1 cup wheat bran
1 cup buttermilk
1/4 cup vegetable oil
1/2 cup brown sugar
1 large egg
1 teaspoon vanilla extract
1 cup all-purpose flour
1 teaspoon baking powder
1/2 teaspoon baking soda
1/2 teaspoon salt
1 cup diced rhubarb (fresh or frozen)
Optional: 1/2 cup chopped nuts (walnuts, pecans), raisins, or dried cranberries

Instructions:

Preheat Oven: Preheat your oven to 375°F (190°C). Line a muffin tin with paper liners or grease the muffin cups.
Soak Bran: In a bowl, combine the wheat bran and buttermilk. Let it soak for about 5-10 minutes until the bran softens.
Mix Wet Ingredients: In another bowl, whisk together the vegetable oil, brown sugar, egg, and vanilla extract until well combined.
Combine Wet and Bran: Add the wet ingredient mixture to the soaked bran mixture. Stir until well combined.
Mix Dry Ingredients: In a separate bowl, whisk together the all-purpose flour, baking powder, baking soda, and salt.
Combine Wet and Dry: Gradually add the dry ingredients to the wet mixture and stir until just combined. Do not overmix; a few lumps are okay.
Add Rhubarb and Optional Add-ins: Gently fold in the diced rhubarb and optional chopped nuts, raisins, or dried cranberries.
Fill Muffin Cups: Divide the batter evenly among the muffin cups, filling each about 2/3 to 3/4 full.
Bake: Place the muffin tin in the preheated oven and bake for about 18-20 minutes, or until the muffins are golden brown and a toothpick inserted into the center comes out clean.
Cool and Pack: Once the Rhubarb Bran Muffins are done, remove them from the oven and allow them to cool in the tin for a few minutes. Then, transfer the muffins to a wire rack to cool completely before packing them in your kid's lunchbox.
Pack in Lunch Box: Once the muffins are completely cool, pack them in your kid's lunchbox. These muffins offer a delicious and fiber-rich snack or breakfast option.
These Rhubarb Bran Muffins are a wonderful way to incorporate the unique flavor of rhubarb into a wholesome and tasty treat. They provide the goodness of bran, fruits, and nuts. Remember to consider any allergies or dietary preferences your child might have while preparing the recipe.

Apricot and chia balls

Ingredients:

1 cup dried apricots, soaked in warm water for 10 minutes and drained
1/2 cup rolled oats
1/4 cup chia seeds
1/4 cup shredded coconut (plus extra for rolling)
1 tablespoon honey or maple syrup
1 teaspoon vanilla extract
Pinch of salt

Instructions:

Soak Apricots: Place the dried apricots in a bowl of warm water and let them soak for about 10 minutes. Drain the soaked apricots.
Blend Ingredients: In a food processor, combine the soaked apricots, rolled oats, chia seeds, shredded coconut, honey or maple syrup, vanilla extract, and a pinch of salt. Blend until the mixture comes together and forms a sticky dough.
Form Balls: Scoop out small portions of the mixture and roll them between your palms to form small balls.
Roll in Coconut: Roll the balls in extra shredded coconut to coat the surface.
Chill: Place the apricot and chia balls on a plate or tray and refrigerate them for about 30 minutes to firm up.
Pack in Lunch Box: Once the balls are chilled and firm, pack them in your kid's lunchbox. You can use parchment paper or a small container to keep them separate.
Pack in Lunch Box: These Apricot and Chia Balls are a convenient and wholesome snack option for your kid's lunchbox. They offer a balance of natural sweetness, fiber, and healthy fats.
These Apricot and Chia Balls are not only delicious but also packed with nutrients. They can be a great source of energy and satisfy your kid's sweet tooth in a healthier way. Always consider any allergies or dietary preferences your child might have while preparing the recipe.

Corn and Bacon Loaf

Ingredients:

1 cup corn kernels (fresh, frozen, or canned)
1 cup all-purpose flour
1 teaspoon baking powder
1/2 teaspoon salt
1/4 teaspoon black pepper
1/2 cup grated cheddar cheese (or cheese of choice)
1/2 cup cooked and chopped bacon
1/4 cup chopped green onions
2 large eggs
1/2 cup milk
1/4 cup melted butter or oil

Instructions:

Preheat Oven: Preheat your oven to 350°F (175°C). Grease a loaf pan and line it with parchment paper for easy removal.
Prepare Dry Ingredients: In a bowl, whisk together the all-purpose flour, baking powder, salt, and black pepper.
Combine Wet Ingredients: In another bowl, whisk together the eggs, milk, and melted butter or oil until well combined.
Mix Batter: Add the wet ingredients to the dry ingredients and mix until just combined. Do not overmix.
Add Mix-ins: Gently fold in the corn kernels, grated cheddar cheese, chopped bacon, and chopped green onions into the batter.
Bake: Pour the batter into the prepared loaf pan and spread it evenly.
Bake: Place the loaf pan in the preheated oven and bake for about 45-50 minutes, or until the loaf is golden brown and a toothpick inserted into the center comes out clean.
Cool and Slice: Once the loaf is done, remove it from the oven and allow it to cool in the pan for a few minutes. Then, transfer it to a wire rack to cool completely before slicing.
Pack in Lunch Box: Once the Corn and Bacon Loaf is completely cool and sliced, pack it in your kid's lunchbox. This loaf offers a flavorful and savory option for lunch or snack time.
Please note that this modified recipe does not include noodles. If you still wish to include noodles, you might consider adapting a casserole-style dish rather than a loaf to better accommodate the noodle texture. Remember to consider any allergies or dietary preferences your child might have while preparing the recipe.

Salmon Patties

Ingredients:

1 can (14 oz) pink salmon, drained and flaked
1/2 cup breadcrumbs
1/4 cup finely chopped onion
1/4 cup finely chopped red bell pepper
1/4 cup mayonnaise
1 large egg
1 tablespoon lemon juice
1 teaspoon dried dill (or 1 tablespoon fresh dill, chopped)
Salt and pepper to taste
Cooking oil for frying

Instructions:

Prepare the Mixture: In a large bowl, combine the flaked salmon, breadcrumbs, finely chopped onion, finely chopped red bell pepper, mayonnaise, egg, lemon juice, dried dill, salt, and pepper. Mix well until all the ingredients are evenly combined.
Form Patties: Shape the mixture into patties, about the size of a small burger. You can make them whatever size is suitable for your child's lunchbox.
Heat Oil: In a skillet, heat a couple of tablespoons of cooking oil over medium-high heat.
Fry Patties: Carefully place the salmon patties into the hot skillet. Cook them for about 3-4 minutes on each side, or until they are golden brown and crispy.
Drain and Cool: Once the patties are cooked, remove them from the skillet and place them on a plate lined with paper towels to drain any excess oil. Allow them to cool.
Pack in Lunch Box: Once the Salmon Patties are completely cool, pack them in your kid's lunchbox. You can include a small container of tartar sauce or lemon wedges for dipping, if desired.
Pack in Lunch Box: These Salmon Patties are a protein-packed and flavorful addition to your kid's lunchbox. They can be enjoyed warm or at room temperature.
Salmon patties are not only delicious but also a great source of healthy omega-3 fatty acids. They can be enjoyed on their own or served in a sandwich or with a side salad. Always consider any allergies or dietary preferences your child might have while preparing the recipe.

Apple and apricot loaf

Ingredients:

2 cups all-purpose flour
1 teaspoon baking powder
1/2 teaspoon baking soda
1/2 teaspoon salt
1 teaspoon ground cinnamon
1/2 cup unsalted butter, softened
1 cup granulated sugar
2 large eggs
1 teaspoon vanilla extract
1 1/2 cups peeled, cored, and chopped apples (about 2 medium apples)
1/2 cup chopped dried apricots
1/2 cup chopped nuts (walnuts or pecans, optional)

Instructions:

Preheat Oven: Preheat your oven to 350°F (175°C). Grease and flour a 9x5-inch loaf pan or line it with parchment paper for easy removal.
Mix Dry Ingredients: In a bowl, whisk together the all-purpose flour, baking powder, baking soda, salt, and ground cinnamon. Set this dry mixture aside.
Cream Butter and Sugar: In a separate bowl, cream together the softened butter and granulated sugar until the mixture is light and fluffy.
Add Eggs and Vanilla: Add the eggs and vanilla extract to the butter-sugar mixture. Beat until well combined.
Combine Wet and Dry: Gradually add the dry ingredient mixture to the wet mixture, stirring until just combined. Do not overmix.
Fold in Apples, Apricots, and Nuts: Gently fold in the chopped apples, chopped dried apricots, and chopped nuts (if using).
Transfer to Loaf Pan: Pour the batter into the prepared loaf pan and spread it out evenly.
Bake: Place the loaf pan in the preheated oven and bake for approximately 50-60 minutes, or until a toothpick inserted into the center of the loaf comes out clean.
Cool: Allow the Apple and Apricot Loaf to cool in the pan for about 10 minutes, then transfer it to a wire rack to cool completely.
Slice and Pack: Once the loaf is completely cool, slice it into individual portions and pack them in your kid's lunchbox.
Pack in Lunch Box: These slices of Apple and Apricot Loaf are moist, fruity, and lightly spiced with cinnamon. They make a perfect snack or dessert for your child's lunchbox.
This Apple and Apricot Loaf is a delightful treat that incorporates the natural sweetness of apples and the pleasant tartness of dried apricots. Consider any allergies or dietary preferences your child might have while preparing the recipe.

Spinach and cheese muffins

Ingredients:

1 cup all-purpose flour
1 cup whole wheat flour
1 1/2 teaspoons baking powder
1/2 teaspoon baking soda
1/2 teaspoon salt
1/4 teaspoon black pepper
2 cups fresh spinach leaves, finely chopped
1/2 cup grated cheddar cheese (or cheese of choice)
1/4 cup grated Parmesan cheese
1/4 cup chopped green onions
2 large eggs
1 cup buttermilk
1/4 cup olive oil or melted butter

Instructions:

Preheat Oven: Preheat your oven to 375°F (190°C). Grease or line a muffin tin with paper liners.
Mix Dry Ingredients: In a large mixing bowl, combine the all-purpose flour, whole wheat flour, baking powder, baking soda, salt, and black pepper.
Add Spinach and Cheese: Add the finely chopped fresh spinach, grated cheddar cheese, grated Parmesan cheese, and chopped green onions to the dry ingredients. Toss them together until they are evenly distributed.
Whisk Wet Ingredients: In another bowl, whisk together the eggs, buttermilk, and olive oil (or melted butter) until well combined.
Combine Wet and Dry: Pour the wet ingredients into the dry ingredient mixture. Stir until just combined. Be careful not to overmix; a few lumps are okay.
Fill Muffin Cups: Spoon the muffin batter into the prepared muffin cups, filling each about 2/3 full.
Bake: Place the muffin tin in the preheated oven and bake for about 18-20 minutes, or until the muffins are golden brown and a toothpick inserted into the center comes out clean.
Cool and Pack: Once the Spinach and Cheese Muffins are done, remove them from the oven and allow them to cool in the tin for a few minutes. Then, transfer them to a wire rack to cool completely before packing them in your kid's lunchbox.
Pack in Lunch Box: Once the muffins are completely cool, pack them in your kid's lunchbox. These savory muffins are packed with spinach and cheese, making them a nutritious and delicious snack or lunchbox addition.
These Spinach and Cheese Muffins are a tasty way to sneak in some extra veggies into your child's diet. Remember to consider any allergies or dietary preferences your child might have while preparing the recipe.

Wholey guacamole

Ingredients:

2 ripe avocados
1 small tomato, diced
1/4 cup finely diced red onion
1/4 cup chopped fresh cilantro
1 clove garlic, minced
Juice of 1 lime
Salt and pepper to taste
Optional: a pinch of cayenne pepper for a little heat

Instructions:

Prepare the Avocados: Cut the avocados in half and remove the pits. Scoop the avocado flesh into a mixing bowl.
Mash the Avocado: Use a fork to mash the avocado until it reaches your desired level of creaminess. Some people prefer a chunky guacamole, while others like it smoother.
Add Tomato, Onion, and Garlic: Add the diced tomato, finely diced red onion, minced garlic, and chopped cilantro to the mashed avocado.
Squeeze Lime Juice: Squeeze the juice of one lime over the mixture. The lime juice not only adds flavor but also helps keep the guacamole from browning too quickly.
Season: Season the guacamole with salt and pepper to taste. If you like a bit of heat, you can also add a pinch of cayenne pepper.
Mix Well: Gently mix all the ingredients together until they are well combined.
Pack in Lunch Box: Transfer the guacamole to a small airtight container. You can also add a few tortilla chips or veggie sticks, such as carrot and cucumber slices, for dipping.
Pack in Lunch Box: Pack the guacamole container along with tortilla chips or veggies in your kid's lunchbox. Guacamole is not only delicious but also a healthy and nutritious snack.
Guacamole is a versatile and flavorful dip that's packed with healthy fats and nutrients from avocados. It's a great addition to any lunchbox and pairs well with a variety of dippers. Remember to consider any allergies or dietary preferences your child might have while preparing the recipe.

Thank you for choosing to embark on this culinary journey with me and for entrusting me with a small part of your kitchen adventures.

Your support and trust mean the world to me. Every recipe, every technique, and every story shared in this cookbook is a reflection of my passion for food and my desire to bring joy to your tables. Your decision to purchase this cookbook not only encourages me to continue sharing my culinary knowledge but also supports the countless hours of recipe testing, writing, and photography that went into its creation.

Wishing you many happy moments of deliciousness and culinary creativity!

For Zian And Milan, who brings smiles to my face and joy to my heart every day

www.ingramcontent.com/pod-product-compliance
Lightning Source LLC
Chambersburg PA
CBHW081237080526
44587CB00022B/3970